Vic Pickup

The Omniscient
Tooth Fairy

Indigo Dreams Publishing

First Edition: The Omniscient Tooth Fairy
First published in Great Britain in 2023 by:
Indigo Dreams Publishing
24, Forest Houses
Cookworthy Moor
Halwill
Beaworthy
Devon
EX21 5UU

www.indigodreamspublishing.com

Vic Pickup has asserted her right under the Copyright, Designs
and Patents Act 1988 to be identified as the author of this work.
© Vic Pickup 2023

ISBN 978-1-912876-78-5

British Library Cataloguing in Publication Data. A CIP record
for this book can be obtained from the British Library.

Designed and typeset in Palatino Linotype by Indigo Dreams.
Cover design from textile artwork by Alix Souissi.
Printed and bound in Great Britain by 4edge Ltd.

Papers used by Indigo Dreams are recyclable products made
from wood grown in sustainable forests following the guidance
of the Forest Stewardship Council.

For Si

This book fairy
is not original
but she's not

She's a tough
fairy.

Acknowledgements

With thanks to the editors of the following publications and websites, where some of these poems (or versions of them) have appeared: Acumen, Atrium, BBC Berkshire, Creative Writing at Leicester, Dreich, Ink, Sweat & Tears, Nine Muses, Peeking Cat, RiversSide, Runcible Spoon, The High Window and The Poetry Village.

Thanks also to the judges who placed these poems:
'The chicken who saved my children' (winner of the Café Writers competition, 2008), 'Occupation' (shortlisted in the National Poetry Day #speakyourtruth competition, 2019) and 'Him, building me a bookcase' (winner of the Cupid's Arrow Prize, 2020).

I would also like to express my gratitude to my friends in the poetry world who have provided support, encouragement and guidance in the writing of these poems. Thank you also to the wonderful Claire Dyer for her Fresh Eyes and the incredibly talented Alix Souissi for her beautiful embroidery skills featured as the cover artwork.

Also by Vic Pickup:

Lost & Found, Hedgehog Press, 2020
What colour is my brain? (Co-written with Jules Whiting),
Hedgehog Press, 2022

CONTENTS

The Omniscient
Tooth Fairy

Why I love butter beans

Day five and on a new ward they bring me a tray.
Set upon it, bashed silver dishes smelling of warmth
and going home soon.

The porter lifts the lids to reveal two steaming
mounds of beige and I think of the woman in this bed
before me, too tired to tick boxes or consider
what she wouldn't have the appetite to eat. Or maybe
she was from a land where off-white food is a comfort.

Left alone, I taste mash in salt butter pillows,
the synthetic smoothness you only get from mixing
powder with hot water—a delight upon which
nestles a heap of butter beans, smooth-skinned.
Their matt creaminess cleaves to the roof of my mouth.

Perhaps I will eat them every day from now on
in celebration because, just as I finish, they wheel her in,
the special care trolley gleaming.
The doctors lift the lid that conceals her in an oxygen bubble,
like a new toy I'm not allowed to open.

I push the tray from my lap, place slippered feet
gingerly on the sparkling floor, and reach in—
the taste of butter beans on my lips.

puzzling; or her 2 women or just one?

- 9 -

Not like it's supposed to be

My key in the door, a gust of wind
opening to the darkened empty hall,
chill in the air.

No waft of slow cooking; no promise
of a hot dinner and custard pudding
wheeled to my lap.

Still wearing my identity label, I move
through the house, flicking switches,
touching radiators.

I scan the table for flowers, a bottle on ice —
teapot ready to go would do. Perhaps
a row of chevroned cards on the mantle?

But no. The kitchen tiles are cold.
I turn the oven to 180, my reflection vanishes
as the light goes on. It looks cosy in there.

Bangings and bustlings resound
as the children surge in, hurling hats and gloves
onto the floor in a race for the remote.

Husband follows, carting bags like
a bedraggled mule. I take a box of fish fingers
from the freezer, tin of beans off a shelf.

It aches to reach but life goes on, despite
what the midwife says. The sink of scuttled dishes
in greying water can wait.

Down the hall, I ease myself onto the edge of the bed,
and look down at the car seat on the floor,
the little face cocooned in pink swaddle.

Welcome home.

Disappointed expectations

This moment too will be forgotten

Through the foggy bedroom landscape
and a muted dawn chorus
the prospect of another day looms.

Snatched naps
and fearful awakenings
are numbed by a cool breeze.

The perpetual state of weary bouncing
which darkness brings with hushed song
lingers in aching joints.

And of you, sacred, nocturnal child,
all I will take forwards
is the time you placed your hands on my face
and kissed me.

No matter what we
Do, will fall short

Building blocks I

We place them on top of each other,
the letters spelling your name – 1,2,3,4
and so on. We click-clack them together,

build buildings, construct bridges,
stack tall, tall towers. When you say:
Mine's taller than yours, we discuss

what's fair and knowing right from wrong.
You learn that in order to build a tower
that's truly taller than mine you have to start

on a flat surface. Together, we lay a book
as your foundation, organise the blocks in accordance
to colour, image, the way the woodgrain flows.

We convert them to maths aids and props for plays.
We explore gravity, materials, talk about trees and later,
various printing techniques.

We divide, count, share,
build the things we find in our dreams,
are always left needing more.

Whatever we do, no matter
how carefully, there's more
we need to do

not filthy bside

School pickup

You run at me, coat billowing in sudden wind like you're Superman. Only two feet tall and loaded up with PE kit, water bottle, wellies, book bag, bounty of Easter eggs spilling. A yellow folder slips freely, flapping its plastic wings into a puddle. Inside is a cardboard crucifix in drag, emblazoned with sequin hearts and green feathers. I try to pick you up, swing you around like in the films, but you're eighty-first percentile and my back is bad. "*I won!*" you shriek—and in your hand, what was once a chocolate rabbit, prised away until home-time and left on a ledge to reform, has now atrophied into a precious, golden, foil-wrapped turd. It's your prize as undisputed victor — my son, King of the Knights of the Square Table, Godfather of the Playground.

start of thing,
my filthy bgefw.

Yamaha YZF600R Thundercat

The loud rumble diminishes to a drone hum
disappearing down the road, dimming after the junction
around the blind bend, then gone.

You listen for the tiny vibrations your ear can't hear—
standing at the end of the driveway, watching your
small slice of freedom vanish into the breeze.

You're no longer one of the masked men who join
in solidarity, engines singing with a love that no-one else
knows, acknowledgement in the dip of the head on passing.

You step slowly, slump slightly, place your leathers
and boots in the cupboard beside a jumble
of small wellies.

Responsibility is invisible, but too heavy a load for a bike.
Irritations of the day buzz around your head like a stuck fly,
with no way to lift the visor.

But hold on. There will be a time—
there will be another.
It will come to you shining bright and gleaming.

A hand will slam the keys down on the desk,
slide them towards you and say:
Take it, it's yours.

Occupation

I am a real-life flesh and blood climbing-frame,
bit squashy here and there to cushion falls.

I am a human tissue, for snots and snivels and
spillages in general, so feel free to use a sleeve.

I am a bodyguard. I walk in the middle of the road,
shield beings with small legs and no common sense.

I am a silver-service waitress, a veritable tasting menu
delivered to plastic plates and bowls thrice daily.

I am a cheese grater, ketchup squirter,
pudding briber.

I am a cleaner. I carry bottles of Pledge and Milton,
a packet of wet wipes holstered at the ready.

I am a machine. I operate despite breakdowns, meltdowns,
strikes and vandalism—even during infestations of lice.

I am the police. I enforce sharing behaviours,
begrudged courtesies and issue ten-pence fines.

I am a referee. I break-up fights, distribute red cards,
threaten with the bench.

I am an independent adjudicator. I bestow nonsense wisdom
and behave inconsistently—to reflect life in the real world.

I am a voluntary Uber driver. I am a councillor, healer, psychic.
I can see and hear things that aren't even there.

I am a forensic scientist, medic, baggage-handler, dental nurse.
I am a mathematician, statistician, weather girl, dairy cow.

I am the singer of ancient and tragic nursery rhymes.
I am a love-maker, life-giver.

I am a world-class
bottom wiper.

Pulling up weeds

The doctor on night shift was old school,
had put it bluntly, as
                    Nature's way
            of getting rid of the duds.

For some reason, I woke with the urge
to weed.

In new light and gardening gloves
I hitched up my dress
and knelt in the dirt—

pulling young green stems
from the fresh black soil,

welling within.

One Tuesday after tea

I've been two minutes too long,
whirling my hands in the washing-up,
trillions of tiny transportive bubbles
dispersing the tacky grease of an afternoon.

I realise
her sobs and protests at an early bath
have subsided.

Grasping the hallway architrave,
I pull my body around the corner
into the bathroom and find
a child's body floating—

an archipelago of pink islands,
foam breaching
at the base of each smooth mound
                              and bile rises

I grab at her with frantic hands—
her eyes bolt open.

She shrieks, and I breathe again,
our lathers dripping to the floor,
melting into water.

Self Help

humour

I'm reading a book called *Stop Worry*. I worry that there'll be things in there that will make me worry. I worry that if I read it and it doesn't stop the worry, then I'll worry even more. If I do read it and it does work I'm going to have to worry about all those moments lost, years wasted, because I didn't read it sooner, and then I'll hate myself for not having read it before. I worry that though the worry may have stopped, it won't last. It will come back even worse because by then I'll know what life is like without it. I worry I'll never stop worrying. That a book can't help me. That I can't help myself. That I *am* worry and worry is me and if I do read the book and it takes the worry away there'll be nothing left but a space where someone used to be.

Irretrievable

When she was seven, I dropped my daughter's tooth
down the sink. As she cried to The Omniscient Tooth Fairy,
I unscrewed the pipes, each one a perfect slimy **O**
confirming my fears that a piece of her was forever gone—
in the belly of a drifting whale-shark, or worse,
her pale milkiness eroding slowly in the sewer dirt.

grtt mtphr

My mother-in-law brought me a lettuce

Peering from the half-filled depths
of its black pot, one green head, frilly nub.
Nothing much.

We sat it on the windowsill. My husband joked
how long it would last before I killed it.

But against the odds, despite my preoccupation
with things that never come to any good, despite
lack of water, it grew.

Its taproot a hidden fist, unclenching roots
and reaching for what it knew in the dark
would help it grow, make it rich, thrive without
admiration and despite neglect

                                          and then

the slow unfurl of crisp fresh palms,
the lengthening, vein strengthening,
building of ribs, veins spreading up and out

and carrying the water I didn't give it
through each intricately threaded leaf.

No grand displays of bloom and wilt. Just
a quiet green luminescence with each day
of sunlight, each day of rain.

Too good to chop and crunch into a salad.
Too alive with vitamins and light
and breath and busy photosynthesis to be lunch.

Don't underestimate the power of a lettuce.
Don't think high water content implies weakness.
This lettuce gave me life, as she knew it would.

Summer holidays

The sitting room, sweet nectarines,
the children half-naked, absorbed

by the television and dribbling juices
down their chins. Rain drums its fingers

on the glass. The toddler wanders in
a sunhat and nappy—any moment might be

the end of the world. Open the window wide
and smell the wet earth.

Watch the leaves drip.
Hear the zephyr whisper.

We take it in, lick our fingers, sink deep.

Learning

I wanted them to grub in the dirt, pick green stems with pink fingers and blow dandelion clocks at the sky—to know the starling, sloe, the softness of moss, the personal treasures of dawn. So that first day off school, with magnifying glass, plastic macs, boots and snacks, we headed to the woods. Crackling between bracken, bramble and thorn, they ran their hands freely over the body of a fallen tree, escorted a roaming beetle to safety, collected dewdrops in cupped hands.

Back home, we emptied our specimen box, set to work on our chart of holly, oak and hawthorn, the peeling scroll of a silver birch needing staples to pin it down. The thing I had been most pleased to find was a single frond of fairy lace, cow parsley, plucked from the intricate embroidery of a hedgerow. I retrieved the nature book, helped them find the page, ready to choose which name they liked best and copy it in muddled hand—but beside what looked like our sprig in monochrome, the words *hemlock, toxic, poison, Socrates' death.*

And so, in spite of their protests, I scooped up the work, the loose frills and ferns and pushed it all to the bottom of the bin, told them to wash their hands, scrub beneath their nails, watched as they did.

unfinished poem

Safeguarding – things to look out for:

If the pupil is suddenly
withdrawn

If she shies away
from PSHE

If you hear talk
of 'a special event'

If the family requests an authorised absence
just before

or after
the summer holidays

If she comes back and has difficulty
walking, sitting or standing

takes a long time in the toilet;
is somewhat changed

Found poem after a school Powerpoint slideshow

Christmas wish

For Christmas this year I want a spider.
A big one, like the kind you see in zoos.
And the one they told us about when we did Jesus
at school, and King Herod wanted to kill all the babies
so Mary took her baby into a cave
and the spider wanted to help and wove a web
right across the entrance, working all night
spinning lace, all gluey and thick,
and in the dark, the frost came and froze it stiff
like tinsel wire, until you couldn't see past
and it looked like it had been there for a thousand years—
so when the soldiers came looking for the baby to kill
they were fooled. The spider's web was so full
with cold sparkles nobody could ever be in there.

I want a spider like that, who will see him coming
and spin a web that quick at night. Then the frost
will come and make it strong, cast a cloak of invisibility
across her door.

New Year's Eve at Frimley Park Hospital

My feet are cold.
I'm wrapped in a scratchy
NHS blanket
on a transformer wardrobe
that turned into a bed.

My daughter lies next to me,
comfortable, snuffling quietly,
cocooned within the multiple folds
of a crisp white sheet.

She sleeps at last,
her veins full of antibiotics,
to kill the infection
that had her vomiting,
shaking, crying,
doubled over on the toilet
on Boxing Day.

It's nine o'clock.
There's a child
crying somewhere on the ward.

Downstairs the staff in purple scrubs
will be polishing off mince pies
in quiet dread of the first drunk, abused partner,
overdose of the night.

- 28 -

Schnitzel

The schnitzel I bought from Tesco defrosts on the kitchen side and I think of the restaurant with steamed windows where we unwrapped our knitted garments and let the back of our legs feel the warmth of the fire as the waitress placed menus on the split-wood table in the corner, the dull glimmer of Christmas lights beyond us. I remember the inward glow of shared glühwein, sugar crystals on my lips where you missed a spot.
We drank, our words lingered in clouds. Collars raised, scarves knotted, you puffed hot breath into my cupped hands and as the sky grew dark, we watched the gingerbread stall bustle and beer tent spill stag dos, a girl selling popcorn reach a fingerless glove into her glass box for yet another handful. Incense of cinnamon and sweet roasted nuts. At the TV centre, our stretched faces were fur-lined reflections in the thousand shiny spheres, convex worlds glowing red and green in the drip of a giant fir tree. At Checkpoint Charlie, we learned of two sides smashing through walls just to hold hands again—digging underground, flying overground, risking all.
A steaming baked potato heaped with sour cream snow is set down, schnitzel, garlic waft and crunch, green beans bathing in a butter puddle — and you're marvelling at your oval platter of steak and heaped frites. We smile, relieved that we are united in our preference of this to last night's pretentious gastro, where they seated us by the door and did not take our coats, the slop of twenty-euro risotto on a square plate. We chose right tonight: the fire spits, we thaw, hungry, tuck in. And I wonder when will be the right moment for you to retrieve the small box in your coat pocket.

Little did I know

that there was a someone out there –
the North to my South
and he spoke with a Mancunian accent;

that when he was growing his lungs
in an incubator with no one to visit him,
I had yet to come into existence –

I watched the rise and fall of his tiny chest
from the ether –

that when at last I came screaming into this world,
he would be building sandcastles under Blackpool lights
and placing his toys in a box for the third time;

that when I was revising for my GCSEs
he was sitting his A levels, both bowed
before Post It note shutters on cupboard doors –

we'd have the same desk lamp from Argos,
our funnel of light –

that we'd lose our virginities at the same time,
sharing in pain and heartbreak, balancing
the giddy skip of infatuation on a see-saw:

that its base was the Midlands,
somewhere around Loughborough;
that I didn't know what real love was.

How to give up

My grandad was at the kitchen table,
my sister on his lap in red gingham check,
back from school to show him
she could write her name—huge biro letters
striding across the back of an envelope.

She nestled on his knee as he tapped ash into a tray,
leaning away to inhale,
puffing a cloud into the hall.

He returned, his mouth warm and smiling,
arms wrapping around for a gentle squeeze.
Just then she wriggled, knocked his wrist
which sent a bolt of ash into her lap.

The grown-ups raced
to dab hot tears, singed skin.

He turned away at the perfect eye
burnt onto her thigh.

Later, when everyone had gone
he would sort the rubbish in silence,
the edge of everything lit by a cold blue moon,
the tight wrap of cellophane packs
a shining layer in the bin.

The summer after getting winded at school

In the photo I'm in a hoody, scruffy jeans.
My friends are wearing party dresses.
The sun is shining.

I have a gift in my hands —
the sheen of the wrap
reflecting into the lens.

I'm wearing a rucksack,
can tell you what's in it:
bottle of water, tissues,

large pot of Vicks Vapour Rub.
My eyes are still red,
from when I'd smeared great gluey globs

on the walls of my bedroom —
my fingers filling cracks, plastering
with the security of eucalyptus.

In the pocket of my hoody is an oblong shape,
my indispensable packet
of menthol Tunes — whenever we'd stop

at the shop after school, my brother
would buy a Mars bar, my sister, Smarties.
I'd always choose Tunes.

Not because I liked them but because I believed
they would open my airways
if my breathing ever stopped.

Spillage

That day you came home broken—
poured yourself out across the floor
then rose, rickety as a foal, unsure
whether you still counted as a man.
When it was over, we looked
at the mess together, the damage done –
assessed what could be put back together,
what we could afford to throw, then
you, armed with a broom, me, first
with a dustpan and brush and
then a bucket and mop –
we set to in the dark renewing
the tiled surface, surveying the job
we'd not yet got around to doing.

- 33 -

Employment

He would 'gift' me the contents of his toilet bowl –
a fresh, unflushed specimen to start my day.

I'd clean his five bathrooms – the four unused
required cleaning all the same.

He'd take offense at the sight of the bin liner,
just visible at the rim –

he'd draw an arrow on paper
to accompany his Post-It note:

They are there to do a job and remain unseen.
I sympathised.

He had a whole room for his white grand piano,
his sheet music of *Twinkle Twinkle*.

I'd have finished scrubbing the downstairs floors
when he'd stand over me, tell me to start again –

he could see the brush strokes were horizontal.
Vertical this time, he said.

My new fridge

is taller than my head
wider than my wingspan
bigger inside than out.

You could keep a corpse inside
(once you'd cut it in half
and frozen the legs.)

My new fridge/freezer
was a rocket in its former life.
Smooth, sleek, white,
various logos emblazoned
on its aerodynamic sheen.

Brace yourself and wear weighted boots
before you pull open the door —
in tinted visor and factor 50, be prepared
for arctic blast and halogen glare
to bleach your earthly senses.

With gloved hand
enjoy the smooth, seductive glide
of durable plastic, translucent shelves
laboratory clean —
no carrot top fronds
or congealed yoghurt crumble —
everything is exactly where it should be.

If I move the wine rack up
and hold my breath
I can just about fit in

and close the door.

I kissed George Ezra

dream of adultery

in a dream last night.
It was long and slow
and delicious.
We were walking
near the gravel works
and just as we paused
beneath a broccoli oak
I reached my arms
around his neck—
he's taller than he looks—
and kissed him.
I was relieved he
didn't pull away
and that my husband
wasn't awake to see it.

Smiling to myself

She was beautiful
    in a Nordic kind of way

with legs built for hiking
    in extra-long skinny jeans.

She was kind too, inviting
    us PTA newcomers into her home—

I'd never before seen a kitchen
    where the taps and sink fold away
      at a hand clap.

Thank you, she said,
    when I handed her my banana loaf—
      but we don't eat unhealthy food.

She was just being honest, but still
    I felt immense joy when I saw
      her husband on the roadside last week

eating a Magnum with relish.

Free fruit for kids

Tomorrow's birthday girl
asleep in bed,
I make a dash
in the dark
to the big Tesco.

My trolley fills up
with balloons,
hats,
plastic tat for party bags.

As I turn a corner
there's a child
eating an orange
from a box
in the middle of the aisle.

She's really gnawing
at the pith,
cramming-every last
sweet-scented gem
into her mouth
like she's never
eaten one before.

She puts the rind in the bin
then rummages
for another
with dirty fingers.

Jungle

Arthur Suleiman warms his hands
on a fire of bits and pieces,
fighting off the cold in a wasteland
strewn with plastic bags.

No croissants in Calais, not in a camp
where desperation trumps currency.
They plot the same tired tricks.
Smudged faces gulp bowls of weak soup.

Arthur smacks his palm – his focus,
the empty tent to the right,
Iranians who took on the big ships
of the night, and didn't return.

Ten times he's been found
clinging to the underbelly of a lorry
like the marsupial baby
of a detached, steely mother.

On a clear day, the white cliffs glow
above the choppy sea.
A mile for every year of his life.
Vines coil around Arthur's feet as

the monkeys swing by, screaming.

Embankment, A35

The three of them were sent out,
ordered to release their seatbelts,
and climb, keep climbing
higher, away from the roar of rushing air
and destabilising afterblow, the scrub
of tall grasses on bare legs.
Suddenly shivering in t-shirt and summer dresses,
they huddle. I scramble up to lay a picnic rug,
shake out beach towels like flags
in which to wrap them, make them seen.
Later, between fresh sheets,
the eldest says: *We looked like those people—*
the ones on the news. I nod,
acknowledging the same thought,
their familiar forms stranded,
caught up in a maelstrom of oil-smeared
paper towels and crisp packets—
while their father, on his phone below us,
sat in the stalled car. The only place
it was quiet enough to hear.
I turn off the lamp, check the time.
I think of the smallness of my prayers,
the insignificance of our rescue
by a man in a yellow van;
the excessive fear as I watched
an invisible hand rock our car on its wheels
as each truck blew past;
the strangeness felt by any mother
hearing herself tell her children
to climb higher still,
who sees their small faces
for the first time as
somebody other than her.

The longing of Judith Kerr

Very, very tender + many poignant children victims of Holocaust

What if you could give them back
their hats, coats, scarves? Place
a knitted glove onto each small hand.
What if you could return their hair to them,
for plaiting, threading with daisy chains;
pull from the sack the toy train,
hand-carved, and old bear,
a travelling companion – exactly the one,
with a bright blue bow around his neck
frayed from too much love?
What if you could put them all back
into the right hands, find the shoes,
a perfect pair, buckle the feet, all tucked up
in woollen socks? What if you could fill
their cheeks until red and ruddy,
make rounded tums and dimpled legs,
scatter freckles on faces with the touch
of summer, then place in one gloved hand
another, bigger? What if you could give them
a mother; give them back a father too,
smiling down as button eyes look up?
What if they could hold hands and step back
on board the train, this one with red velour seats
and a warm welcome from the lady
with the trolley, who offers jelly sweets
and apples and a storybook,
about a tiger who came to tea?

*Judith Kerr's 'Creatures' (2015) is dedicated to "the one and a half million Jewish
children who didn't have my luck, and all the pictures they might have painted."*

Lipstick

After Lieutenant Colonel Mervin Willett Gonin DSO's diary extract

five hundred a day were dying and would go on dying for
weeks more before anything we could do would change it –

we looked past, seeing the remains as trip hazards, mounds
barely identifiable, to the woman washing in water from a tank
where a child's body floated –

to those relieving themselves of caustic bowels in walkways
using stacks of bodies to stay upright while they waited for
what we gave them to cook on an open fire –

as supplies rolled in we looked upon the boxed lipsticks in
horror, the hundreds of thousands of things we needed more –

I wish I could discover the genius that put them on that order –
I saw women in beds with no sheets or nightgowns, sweeps of
lipstick on their mouths –

women walking the camp in just a blanket, their lips painted
scarlet – a woman on a post-mortem table with a small piece of
lipstick still in her hand –

I wish I could thank that person who gave them something that
made them more than a tattooed number, ignited a flicker of
identity, a thin layer of dignity –

the beginning of giving them back their humanity.

The chicken that saved my children

Thanks be to Hašmeta, the chicken
who came home with us in place of Sofia's wedding ring.
She made do with a hard and dirty yard for her home
and as she scuffed and pecked and jutted
the hills sent bullets, the sky's moan was shrill.
Hašmeta, swivelled her head and saw my children crying
—alas, no egg would come. We saved food,
Nada and Almir grew thin; their cheeks were hollow,
not fat as children's faces ought to be. Hašmeta saw this.
She worried so, her feathers grew thin.
She picked at herself, hateful for the lost gold.
She stopped clucking those comforting noises,
fretted and shook with each impact.
One day, I took Hašmeta a slice of somun
and noticed a beautiful thing tucked into the corner.
Hašmeta scratched the floor, puffed her chest.
Sofia heated the pan on the stove.
The children gathered to see the orange and white bubble,
the edges becoming crisp and brown.
Sofia and I watched as they mopped the liquid gold,
licked their lips, made lovely smacking noises.
Their eyes grew bright, their faces warmed.
They stroked Hašmeta every day. Nada sometimes sang.
We told her we would defend her forever, we would never
harm her, we would never let them take her.
When shelling was heavy we even brought her inside.
Soon she began to cluck again. Each day we would have one,
sometimes two perfect eggs.
We were the only family that remained whole
when the Chetniks came down from the hills.
Thanks be to Hašmeta, the chicken that saved
my children.

In Churchill's

The boy in the fish and chip shop
once felt sad enough to slice
the soft white skin
on the inside of his wrist.

He has a thick scar
shining wide and purple
like a fat worm sliding up his sleeve.
You'll see a flash of it

as he deftly shovels and shakes,
the shimmering fish and chips
in air that sparkles
with hot oil spit
and running salt.

He hands me three warm bundles,
each triple-wrapped
with thick folds
neatly tucked.

Frass ?

Woodworm

enjambe poem

What started with a single hole
just above your eyebrow
like where a nail had been
we soon realised bored deeper
began to repeat itself
in an irregular pattern of cruel symmetry

and so   while you slept
we looked inside to find you
        riddled —

a tangle of tunnels beneath your crust
leading to vast empty halls
with rice paper walls
and dormant wasp nest cities

We gently held the halves back together
watched the holes unite and crumble

and now each day I sit
blow and brush the frass clear
with my fingertips
stroke the skin that once stroked mine —

a downy bare peach
worlds building within

How children
react to suffering

Shame

After school each week
I would hide amongst the lipstick walls
sampling my own natural blusher hues
as my mates assembled outside
the newsagent next door
in their bubble gum burst,
Coke and Chuppa Chup haze

I crouched down in the aisle
amidst the rows of Impulse and Immac
muttering silent prayers
as my mother collected
yet another multipack of
incontinence pads

that the *toocoolforschool* kids
would not come in or see us
through the wall of glass
or know the meaning of *Staydry*

or know about my ailing grandfather
in the next village
in his penultimate bed
Grandad farmer soldier veteran
whose wife talked of angels
who'd help her turn him in his sheets
and balm the sores that kept him awake

while I hid from the world
between nail polish shades
of plush pink and aqua marine
hoping one day these trips would stop

It's late when I realise I've forgotten to do your meds

There's a jangle of keys on the ring, but I know just the one.

As I slot it into the eye
      I'm home from school,
      back from a night out, mouth alcopop-sweet
         and the juice of ash from club carpets
         coating the straps of my stilettos;
      Home for Christmas, Chris Rea all the way,
         casserole bubbling, steam on the window,
         cat on the tinselled ledge;
      seeking refuge
         when I didn't want to put up a fight.

As I turn it and gain entry
      the tinsel's there,
         my husband put it up yesterday;
      the floor's been cleaned, a faint whiff of bleach.

As I switch on the light and, squinting, retrieve the tray
      of cartons and brown bottles, the many open
      mouths of a colour-coded pill box, waiting
      for me to fill them, click the lids safely shut.

Tell me,

how do I colour a unicorn mid-flight and bake butterflies
nestled into vanilla cream, indulge in their sweetness

and close my eyes to the bra strap you cannot fasten, the pain
relief providing none, that jams your digestive system shut—
how do I flush the toxins out?

How do I save the memory of your perfume buried in folds of
soft wool around your neck, fresh sheets after sickness, melon
boats with sliced orange sails and a red cherry crow's nest?

How do I cherish the soft baby down of *my* making,
small fingers and half-moons peeping, warm milk
with marshmallow clouds floating in our skies?

How do I comfort their nightmares of monsters and spiders
and *your* nightmare of silence

and remember amidst all that, to keep receipts, self-examine
monthly, eat avocado and oily fish, breathe in deep and hold?

Old Cleopatra

Her face is parchment, royal jelly collecting in the creases
of her brow, kohl spider's legs retreat from loose-lidded eyes.

Elephants' feet raise her up, but still any paid-for visitor can see
she's shrunken in the chair, pop-socks not quite reaching the
hem of her skirt.

She never hears from her sons; doesn't know if they lived or
died. On occasion, her daughter sends flowers. Still no word
from Antony.

Without milk for her powerbath, she makes do with rose water,
almond oil, slips a note in a porter's pocket when the bottles
run dry.

She laments henna-licked nails and red ochre lips,
the crease of her bust in gold plate—her strong, swan neck.

Now sockets grind like stone. She leans forward, tries to reach
for the asp—

but the snake sleeps on undisturbed, coiled neatly
behind her armchair.

Building Blocks II—
Minecraft

They build scenes of their own creation
with blocks of discerning colour:

A pigsty with pink squealing cuboids
frantically snuffling, hovering in mid-air.

A lava lake glimmer, the screen too hot to touch.
Rainbow waterfalls, rectangles rippling mirrors.

Through some technological miracle they occupy
each other's worlds. They always play by the rules.

They talk in code, launch into fantastical tales
of what has happened today in a separate realm to mine.

There's a man in Germany, they say, who managed
to hide and stay hidden for eight whole years.

Nobody found him, not even the zombies. That man
is a legend, a hero in their eyes, in a world

from which I am already excluded.

a sense of
time passing

University car park

Beneath floodlights, on AstroTurf
they chase the ball in clinging shorts,

thighs thick with muscle
like meat carved into joints.

While I was birthing babies
they were running in playgrounds,

their knees like elbows,
white foal legs tripping.

Now they gallop and conquest like wild beasts,
chest pelts slick. They shout and gesture as

                              I stand
with my car keys in a gloved hand,

feeling the tarmac beneath my shoes thump
in time with their studded boots.

Steam rises into the night.
There is a nip in the air, promise of frost—

the shock of ice
a hardened plate of glass.

Facts of life

The world is in on a joke
even the lines on the playground understand.

So I buy a book
and we sit on her bed to talk

about hormones, bras, penises,
and preventing the miracle of life.

There's the question of the *animal blood*
she once saw in the bathroom.

My reassurance there had been no slaughter —
that's what it is to be woman.

Afterwards, I smooth the sheets.
Teddies gather, not knowing their place.

In the morning, it's hairbrush, uniform, water bottle.
Sandwich and apple placed in her unicorn bag.

She waves as she turns the corner.
The sun is out. The day is cold.

Him, building me a bookcase

Sixteen chunky shelves, propped on blocks
of pallet wood, sliced like angel cakes –
each one a different shade.

A dusty finger pins the glossy pages
of a how-to book. Cautiously, he drills,
but soon his eye is fixed, unblinking.

The bar turns, the wood secured in its vice.
Lines of sinew flicker in his forearm as he saws,
then blows and smooths the debris clear.

He measures with one eye shut,
improvises in places where
the spirit level would not go.

He gives purpose to timber fit only for the fire,
a hand-me-down drill and screws
from an ice cream tub on a garage shelf.

Having masked the edges, he applies three coats,
wearing war paint of magnolia, the glean of cream
laden thickly on his brush.

We stand and my hand slides
into his back pocket, already wondering
which will go where and in what order.

He doesn't know, but this is my greatest wish:
not the having of a place
or a way to keep things, only this –

Him, building me a bookcase.

Conversation with a cavewoman

No, we don't get many sabre-toothed tigers,
food stores are reasonable at our local Tesco Extra,
my partner has no need for a spear or knife –
he uses a thing called a Mac to sustain his brood,
and firelighters, individually wrapped.

I have not lost any children to the cold or hunger –
nobody wants to take them in the night or kill them.
My milk didn't dry up in a drought.
When our son had a cough we drove to the A&E in town
and didn't have to wait long.

But I lie awake at night,
I dread what I cannot stop,
My inability to forage, find fresh water or control my fears,
that my children will live like me, speak like me
be frightened of this world.

I worry I don't show love as other people do
that they will need pills or to pay someone
just to talk.
On days when the cloud-base is low, and the list
of what's needed unravels, as I so frequently do,

I want to swaddle their skins
in animal fur, smother them with my scent
have enough fuel to keep the fire strong
and the glow in their faces, knowing
I can take on the world.